Baby Juan -
 To my g[randson?]
others to [...]
your "you"
you the unique person that y[ou are...]
 Wish on a star, walk on a moonbeam
dance on a rainbow and don't be
afraid to dream. If you stay committed
to your dreams they will become a
reality.
            Peace & Blessings
            Lisa Tovar
            3/29/14

EPIPHANIES

Kim,
 The inscription is
for Juan when he
grows up and is
able to read and
understand it. So
that means you guys
have to hold on to it
for him. ☺ Love ya,
                Lisa

"Epiphanies"

1. *A literary work or sections of a work presenting such a moment of revelation and insights.*

2. *Any situation in which an enlightening realization allows problems or situations to be understood from a new and deeper perspective.*

EPIPHANIES

Next Step Writers
And
Truth in Us Writers Groups

Reflections Publishing House

Epiphanies
Next Step Writers Groups
Truth in Us Writers Group

2014 © Reflections' Creative Writers Workshop Series

Printed in the United States of America.

All rights reserved.
No part of this book may be reproduced
without the written permission of the contributing authors
First Printing, March 2014

ISBN 978-0-9792132-4-3
Library of Congress Control Number: 2014902246

Reflections Publishing House
Inglewood, CA
reflectionspublishings.com

Cover art by Deborah Bellis and
Clark Graphics

Contents

Acknowledgments 7

Introduction 13

Isabelle Gunning 15

   Evidence is Emotional 17

   Clients Teach 21

Rita Hall 29

   Friends for Life 33

Darla Jackson 41

   The Call 43

   Expression of Love 52

   Choices 53

Beverly Hyman Reynolds 55

   Mama Afterwards 57

   Leaving Houston 67

   The Seven Minute Story 73

Pamela Snowden 79

   Lost and Found 81

   Affirmations 88

Mel Taylor	91
We Walked With Tears in Our Eyes	93
Lisa Tovar	99
The Skin That I Am In	101
Paula White	109
So Not Stupid	111
Deborah Bellis	119
Hit it	121

Acknowledgments

ISABELLE GUNNING

First I would like to thank God — the Mother-Father Creative Power and Presence that lives and moves as all things. I am grateful for this Divine Power and Presence in me.

I also want to thank my life's partner, Pam. Her love and support in all aspects of my life is always appreciated--even if I do not tell her often enough.
I am especially grateful for her suggestion that we both pursue our dreams of writing by joining the Next Step Writers Group.

I also want to acknowledge my mother, Nella, who has been living a life of humor, strength, determination and faith for 99 years, and my daughter Jolanda, who has been living a life of humor, brilliance, beauty and strength for 26 years. Both of them are tremendous sources of inspiration for me.

I am grateful to all the members of my fellow Next Step Writers Group. It has been a joy and inspiration to be around such creative genius, and I appreciate all the constructive criticism and support. I also thank those members of the Truth in Us Writers Group who joined us Next Step Writers in this project. Our time together was brief but powerful and inspirational.

I also want to thank Reflections Publishing. I am grateful to Mel Taylor who let Spirit move through him to invite me to participate with this wonderful group of writers and to start on this magnificent writer's journey. And more gratitude than I can express goes to the incomparable Deborah Bellis. Her wisdom and enthusiasm has made all the difference in my willingness to step up and be the writer Spirit intended for me to be.

RITA HALL

First and foremost I want to thank my Heavenly Father for the life He gave me and the gifts He has deposited within me. Lord, help me to use my gifts to honor you and the plans you have for me. Jeremiah 29:11 next I want to honor my ancestors whose DNA flows through my veins. I celebrate all of you; known and unknown. You gave me the strength not to give up in the face of adversity. You taught me to have integrity and to stand up for who and what I believe in even if it is not the popular point of view. You said that taking an unpopular stand might cost me upward mobility, but it was the right thing to do. You told me to pray for the wisdom to know which battles to fight and which ones to walk away from, thank you Mom (Muzet H. Hall) for all the lessons and memories we shared. Thank you for showing me how to die with dignity and grace. I hope that when it comes my time to transition I can be as brave and peaceful as you.

EPIPHANIES

Aunt Edna and Uncle Wash thank you for instilling character and morals in me. Cousin A D, thank you for proving that a great sense of humor is a valuable trait to have and that it is a universal language. Finally, I dedicate this story to the millions of people who have dreams and goals, especially to the children. Never, ever, ever give up on your dreams. Never allow anyone and I do mean anyone to steal, derail, detour or destroy your dreams. Hold them close; they are precious. Believe in yourself, have faith and passionately pursue your dreams. If you can believe it, you can achieve it. *Blessings and Miracles.*

DARLA JACKSON

It is with much love that I acknowledge those in my life who support me unconditionally. Thank you to Charles, Shameika, Louise and my entire family for believing in my ability to achieve my highest goals. I also give a special thank you to my grandmother Piccola who nurtured me and gave me the foundation that led me to believe in myself. Also, special thanks to Reflections Publishing House and the Next Step Writers.

BEVERLY HYMAN REYNOLDS

My love and thanks to my family and friends who, for several years, listened patiently to my intentions of getting my stories published; to my professors who encouraged me to become a writer; and especially to Debbie Bellis of Reflections Publishing House whose talent, writing workshops, and support got these stories from my head and heart into print.

PAMELA SNOWDEN

My family has given me love, support and encouragement in all aspects of my life, including my writing. Isabelle, my life partner, brought me with her to church on the fateful day that marked the beginning of my spiritual rebirth and renaissance. Isabelle blazed the spiritual path for me. I am grateful to her for that, and also for never having said "I told you so." Jolanda, our daughter, is and has been a continuing source of pride and joy, as well as my lifeline to the twenty-first century!

The ministerial education program at One Spirit Interfaith Seminary in New York City has been an answered prayer for me. I wanted an ordination program that was intellectually rigorous, independent of formal organized religion and made provisions for distance learning students. One Spirit provided me with all those things and more. I am grateful to the staff and students at One Spirit, all of whom walked with me on my path to ordination. Deborah Bellis and her Next Step Writers Workshop have been blessings to me. Deborah is a knowledgeable and gifted teacher, and she has imparted broad knowledge, technique and inspiration in equal measure. Reflections Publishing House has made it possible to move from wishful thinker to published author. Thank you.

LISA TOVAR

My heartfelt thanks to my family members and friends who were there when I needed them; Brian, Reynaldo, Christopher, Charro, Amber Tovar, Desmond Rivers and Candis Carew. Victoria Potlongo, Rita Hall, Paula Manley, Char Branch, Linda Lee, Roslyn Alexander, Andrea Roundtree and Jo-An Allen-Turman, you are all my earth angels! A special note of gratitude and appreciation is owed to Deborah Bellis, for her encouragement and support. In loving memory of my parents; Estaban & Cordelia Tovar whose wisdom, spirit, and guidance still linger within me. And in honor of my late husband, the love of my life, my friend, my rock, Laurence T. Carew, who loved me for the person that I am.

PAULA WHITE

First I need to acknowledge God. If not for his arm around my shoulder and his hand over my big mouth at just the right times, there's no way I could've made it this far. In writing this story, I remembered things that I had spent most of my life trying to forget. If anyone's feelings have been hurt, my apologies. To my mother, I believe you loved me the best you knew how. I just wish I had the courage to tell you how much I was hurting, to my father, thanks for giving me life, love and identity.

EPIPHANIES

To my children, Mister and Mia, thank you both for giving me joy and a purpose. Thank you for accepting all my many mistakes and loving me in spite of them. I am so very proud of you both and want only the best for you. To my friends Kat, Roz, Danielle, and Janice, thank you all for the good times, the crazy times and the times I'm still trying to figure out. You have helped mold me into the friend I now know how to be. To B.K., you taught me to always give my best and that it didn't matter where I started, the important thing is where I ended up. Save a spot for me in heaven. You'll never be forgotten.

To Dickie, you were a true soldier. You took a chance and gave me a job when no one else would. You made me believe that all things are possible. I forgive you for listening to the haters. You are missed and loved. To Poppa, you have been a constant bright spot in my life since the day you convinced me to allow you in my life. Lol your commitment and dedication to me has touched my heart like never before. I love you without limits.

Clyde Terry, thank you for your patience, knowledge and strength. Mike aka Party Mike for being the official good dude. Last but not least, to all those who were treated in a way that made them feel less than perfect. Only your thoughts and actions will determine who you really are. Remember God doesn't make mistakes. We are the people God meant us to be and that makes us perfect.

Introduction

I'm excited, watching the members of Truth in Us and Next Step Writers turn themselves into a solid and steadfast group of writers. They are a lively bunch, who lives with God, full of vision and purpose, reaching and striving for the high call in their lives.

They move along a path that they create for themselves. A course that swerves, dips and zig-zags, but a passageway that is sturdy as they remain true to the visions that they have birthed in the writers' workshop. Epiphanies is a perfect title for this group of writers.

I'm walking to school with Lisa as she faces racism from her own people. I shout with joy, watching Pam walk proudly across the stage to her ordination. Darla encourages me, as I witness her release when she found her writers' voice. I'm in the classroom with Isabelle, as she encourages her students to greatness. Rita's story reminded me of the lifelong bond of sister friends. Mel wrote about an historical time long gone, but not forgotten. I visualize the supernatural dreams Beverly has about her mother, and I cheer Paula on when she discovers who she really is.

EPIPHANIES

These writers write with a sense that something is changing, and they transform, just like a caterpillar morphs into a beautiful and colorful butterfly. Their stories are powerful, emotional and written so naturally that there is no doubt that they are on their way to becoming successful authors in their own right.

Epiphanies is an immensely gripping anthology that inspires us to overcome, celebrate our accomplishments and share the nurturing power of good and solid storytelling.

Reflections Publishing House is honored to present this impressive and poignant work to you. Come, take a peek, look into the spirit of the writers, share the adventure, and drink deeply from our living wells of life.

Deborah Bellis
Publisher/Facilitator

Isabelle Gunning

Is a creative writer interested in having her stories be a source of entertainment and spiritual uplift. She teaches law and conflict resolution, and is a licensed spiritual counselor who enjoys being of service to others. She likes to read, play with her dogs and cats, have adventures with her partner Pam and brag about their daughter's many successes. She can be reached at: isawrites@aol.com.

Evidence is Emotional

Isabelle Gunning

"My people," I spoke a little louder. I didn't think they heard me the first time. "I need at least one volunteer." My request was met with silence; *I wonder why nobody's answering?*

I always looked forward to my Advanced Evidence Class. The students were actually interested in evidence and trial work...rather than taking the basic evidence class just because it is a subject on the Bar Exam that all potential lawyers must pass in order to practice law. The students in this class were always excited, ready to work.

Oh, sometimes I forget that my students have never tried a murder case.

EPIPHANIES

It started as a normal class. I started out the way I normally do with these students. Not begging for anyone to speak, but choosing among enthusiastic participants. "All right, any volunteers for getting Peoples Exhibit A through D admitted?" "What will you say to the judge?"

Silence

That surprised me. Where were my high-energy young lawyers-to-be? Hands up. Ready to out-do each other? I decided I'd better call on someone.

"Eric, come on down."

Eric got up slowly from his seat; he seemed reluctant to come to the front of the practice court-room. I was surprised. Eric is my eager beaver. He's the guy who dresses in a suit, complete with matching tie and pocket kerchief — when he knows he will be doing a practice direct or cross examination of a witness to make sure he sounds and looks the part of a lawyer.

Eric spoke softly "Your Honor may I approach the witness?"

I looked down on him from my elevated judge's seat. I was intent on teaching my students the process of admitting evidence in a trial — in this case the pictures of the charred and blackened bodies of the two children trapped in the building the defendant in our hypothetical case had set on fire. Although, the classroom case was based on a real arson case I had tried. The pictures or exhibits we were using for our evidence were copies of some of the real black and white photos from that case. I pulled my black imitation judge's robes around me.

"Of course, Counselor" I said in my role as the mock/fake judge.

"Officer Murray, I am showing you pictures of…."
His voice cracked. "Excuse me…I mean…I am showing you a picture of what has been previously marked as…" He stopped. He looked down at the pictures and then turned his head away. He broke out of his lawyer character.

"Professor this is horrible! These pictures are sickening." "They are pictures of dead children, really dead, this is all so emotionally exhausting." "How can you do this?"

And so we stopped. The picture of my strong, eager, tough, students collapsed. I needed to start over — this time, remembering that my students had never tried a murder case.

My unlimited potential meets every demand in new and expanded ways.

Clients Teach

Isabelle Gunning

I opened the door to New Faith Baptist, a modest one-room store-front church, with mixed emotons. Even from the door, I could see him in the cheap coffin. *He's really dead.* And, although a part of me wanted to "shush" the unattractive feeling welling up in me, I felt it — Relief.

Memories of Mr. Washington Pettus flood to me. He was not much taller than me and relatively small for a man. He always wore dark pants. They appeared to be made of strong material — and seemed permanently embedded with dirt and sweat. He always wore a dark suit jacket, but not one that matched his pants. On his head, he wore a black plastic derby hat which pressed his long Afro down to his ears and neck.

But what I remember most was his yelling. Yelling for me in the hallways of our public defender offices....long before he got to my office. And yelling at me when he finally saw me.

"What have you done on my case, Miss Lawyer? You seem to be slow."

"Mr. Pettus," I would say with a deep sigh, "You were just here yesterday so there has not been much for me to do since then. You have been charged with trespass and..."

"Miss Lawyer, Miss Lawyer! Did you really go to law school?" He interrupted. "I told you that that apartment is mine. I was born and grew up there. Now how could I trespass on my own place? Do you really know the law?"

I hated it when he would accuse me of not knowing the law or of not being a lawyer. I was a young black woman lawyer and too often people in the courthouse would assume that I was a juvenile defendant's mother looking for the right court room. I didn't need a client I had been working hard to help to claim, loudly, that my credentials and skills were bogus.

Mr. Pettus. As I told you, I investigated the property records and spoke to the current owners. Unfortunately, you were evicted from the property almost a year ago when the new owners bought the building from your old landlord. They have turned the building into medical office space..."

"They can't do that Missy. That is my home. Have you read the Constitution of the United States? It says I have the right to property. Not just the big shots but us little guys. We have rights too. Maybe I need a new lawyer!"

I walk down the short aisle of the church to view his body: I remember when the conversation turned to his getting a new lawyer. Alone at his coffin — not even the small church's minister was there, I stood looking at his body and getting lost in my memories.

The thought of being replaced as his lawyer delighted me. Mr. Pettus' case was just a misdemeanor—if he were convicted; he couldn't get more than a year in jail. It was clear to me when I spoke with the owners – a delightful young professional couple trying to provide health care for a working class African American community—that Mr. Pettus had broken into his old apartment many times. They felt sorry for the guy. Even, Steve Johnson, the prosecuting attorney handling the case, and a man I normally did bitter battle with over every case we faced each other over, was actually sympathetic.

"Hey Miss Lawyer," Steve said when he called me to discuss the plea offer.

"Steve. Don't call me that." I said.

He laughed. "Sorry. I heard your client calling you that and I thought...."

"You thought it was funny but it is not."

"Okay, okay. Look I know I tend to be hard on most of your clients who are just thugs in my view. But this guy is just nuts. Find him a place to live and let him plead to the one trespass charge and I will agree with you that the guy should do no time, just probation only; now that's fair."

"Steve as you know, I never agree with you on what is fair or not. But...as usual I will speak with my client."

Of course it was a fair offer. But my problem was convincing my client.

"Plead? As in plead guilty? Like I did something wrong?" Mr. Pettus was screaming in my office. He was so loud that other attorneys, investigators and secretaries came down the hallway, peeking into my office to see what was going on. Most smiled. The trouble client.

EPIPHANIES

"Mr. Pettus I have already spoken with New Horizons. It's a great place for people who like yourself don't have a place to live. And we are in luck because Ms. Maisha, the director of New Horizons, told me they have a bed for you. It can be very hard to get a bed; and they will help you find another apartment."

"I don't need another apartment! I have one. What I need is another lawyer. A real lawyer. One who knows the law."

Standing silently at his coffin, I thought, he will never scream at or berate me again. Relief. But something else too. I heard a noise and saw the church pastor.

"Welcome, Sister, welcome. Mr. Pats uh Petty hasn't had any visitors so it's great to see you. How did you know him?"

"Mr. Pettus. And he was my client."

"Oh well, right. We here at New Faith Baptist try to help whenever there is one who has no one to mourn or bury them. We do what we can. At least get a coffin and say a few words of prayer before he gets buried. Will you stay for the service? It won't be long." *Stay for the service?* I thought back on the day in open court when the judge heard Mr. Pettus' motion to remove me as his lawyer.

A courtroom is a space designed so that people can be heard. Everyone in the room should be able to hear the judge, the witnesses, and the attorneys—every time they speak. Fortunately for me, the day Mr. Pettus's motion to remove me was heard; there were not a lot of spectators. But it was far from empty. The judge had left the motion for the last case on his docket.

The clerk announced, "The case of the People versus Washington Pettus. All parties and counsel please come forward."

There I was with Mr. Pettus. Steve was at the other end of the counsel table.

Judge said, "Mr. Pettus you have a motion here. You are unhappy with your lawyer?"

"Yes, Your Honor. I don't think she understands the law or the Constitution. She is just not what I need…." He rambled on. His black plastic derby sat slightly askew on his head.

Steve was snickering. A few of my colleagues from my office were in the courtroom supposedly for support---but their suppressed laughter was no comfort. The clerk was shaking with mirth. Only

EPIPHANIES

the judge beamed compassion at me with his blue eyes while he nodded politely as my client ranted on.

To my relief, the judge finally stopped him, "Mr. Pettus, I really appreciate your concerns. But I can assure you that you have an excellent lawyer. You will not find a better one in this courthouse. So I'm sure that you have just had a misunderstanding and I will ask you to keep trying to work things out with her. Thank you sir, thank you counsel," the judge said, dismissing us.

And so I was stuck with Mr. Pettus, until the call came saying that he had died. No information on how or why — just that he was dead. And instead of being in court with him, I was here at New Faith Baptist, at his funeral.

The door to the church swooshed open bringing a swatch of light and Maisha from New Horizons, into the darkened interior.

"Hey girl," she greeted me warmly. "I'm glad you are here. No one tends to show up at these services that New Faith Baptist does for homeless people. They don't have anybody. So I try to come when I can. And he was almost one of our clients."

"True," I murmur, "If only he had been."

"Yeah, living on the streets is deadly." I went out to talk with him in that alley he stayed in a couple of times to try to get him to come to New Horizon. But...But he did have you. You know he talked about you. 'My lawyer' he would say with pride. "

"He talked about me?"

"Oh Yes. Of course he did say he had to "school you" on things. But he was happy to have someone fighting for him. "

Fighting for him? I wonder now if I fought hard enough. I was always so frustrated with him. But, in truth, I had done all a lawyer could do. Perhaps, I could have been a better friend, a more compassionate witness to his misguided attempts to stand up for himself.

My eyes glistened as I took Maisha's arm and we walked together to take our seats for the service. Not crying but I shed a few tears for my "trouble client." I knew he was finally safe and at peace now. He made it home, to a place where he didn't have to fight to stay there. Sitting there, I felt grateful because my heart is bigger and stronger because I had Mr. Pettus in my life.

Baby Juan,
Enjoy the read!
Rita

3/29/14

Rita Hall

EPIPHANIES

Rita Hall

Has always loved the art of storytelling, and as a small child she had a vivid imagination. She was able to weave stories that kept other children and adults spell-bound for hours with her animated stories, her first book, *Ebony Bitter-Sweet, a Chocolate Girl in a Vanilla World* is a collection of poetry and prose which touches the heart and warms the soul. She is a contributing author to the following on-line magazines: *Foray, Joy Comes, and Independent Voices*. Rita is a Motivational Speaker who speaks at schools from K thru College level to encourage youth to set goals and pursue their dreams. She has a Master's degree in Negotiations and Conflict Re-solution and Emergency Services Administration. Rita is the Co-Founder and President of Holy Helping Hands

EPIPHANIES

Non-profit. This organization assists foster care youth with scholarships. They provide services to U. S. Veterans at the VA Hospital and they help recovering female substance abusers. Rita is also the co-founder along with Dr. Anita Moultrie, of Twin Hope. This organization is committed to the empowerment of youth. Rita recently created a line of bath and skin care products (*Diva My Way*). Now, Rita is taking the foray into writing a novel. One of her favorite genres of books is the mystery. Rita's novel, *Badge of Honor* is a Christian murder mystery. It promises to be both thrilling and filled with many plot twists. Look for it in 2015. You can contact Rita at RitaHallAuthor@aol.com and (323)863-3747.

My steps are ordered by God. Everything I am or ever hope to be is due to his grace and mercy.

Friends for Life

Rita Hall

The song kept drifting through my head; *Make new friends, but keep the old. One is silver and the other's gold.* I learned this song in the Girls Scouts as a Brownie and it still rings true fifty years later. Lorraine and I were enjoying taking a stroll back down memory lane. Some memories were hysterical and we laughed till we cried.

I was in Atlanta for a business seminar. However, if I am anywhere near the Atlanta area, I never miss an opportunity to spend time with my best friend from childhood. Lorraine and I had been friends since she was ten and I was eleven. We met in the sixth grade at Angeles Mesa Elementary School.

EPIPHANIES

"Lorraine, do you remember how many people predicted that you and I would be barefoot, pregnant and on welfare? They said that because we were from broken homes with absent fathers' that we would have loose morals and never amount to anything."

But on a lighter note, Lorraine and I laughed at all the adults and peer naysayers we had encountered in our lives. Her husband Ken who had joined us for dinner marveled at how even after fifty years she and I are still extremely close friends.

"Do I ever! But here is the hysterical part, we beat the odds girl. And we beat them well. We did not have children out of wedlock or dabble in drugs like some of the ones predicted to succeed."

"Yes we did, we beat the hell out of the odds Lorraine. We showed them that we could achieve even with obstacles; no fathers present, little money only a desire and a dream to succeed. Also, they must not have known how much you and I love shoes. Girl, at the very least I knew that we would never be barefoot," and we both laughed again. "But I do remember being angry that adults would say that we were doomed. They should have been encouraging us to be all that we could instead of tearing us down. To this day I wish I could find my history teacher who said I wouldn't turn out to be anything. For years when I was on patrol, I prayed to stop his car for a moving violation and issue him a ticket, with a *how you like me now attitude.* "

"Rita, I remember when the conversations in sociology class would arise about whether nurture or environment played the most important role in how an adult turned out. As the class debated the issue, I posed the following questions to my professor. "What about the innate deep down desire to succeed? What about determination and tenacity? What role do these factors play in human development?" "Let me guess Lorraine, the professor was not prepared to discuss *that* point of view?" Back then, if it was not in the text book, it was not discussed."

"Correct."

"Well, I think that we can provide an answer on nature vs. nurture."

"Rita, you are right. For us nature and nurture was not nearly as important as our faith in God, believe in self and having someone else to both believe in you and hold you accountable."

Lorraine now has her law degree and is working in a very demanding, but rewarding career. She was able to go straight through college with no breaks and graduate on time as scheduled.

EPIPHANIES

My story is slightly different. While going to college, I had to drop out at the beginning of my junior year for financial reasons and join the workforce. I remember the naysayers surfaced again with, "Aha, I told you so. I knew that *both* of them would not succeed." That was a very painful time for me. Leaving school before graduation was not something I had anticipated. I was devastated and felt like a failure. After throwing myself a pity party, I had to snap out of it. I had to refocus and get my head back in the game.

Although I had to drop out of college, Lorraine *always* believed in me. She *never* doubted that I would someday return and finish my degree. I remember that she got into some pretty heated debates with some of our Delta sorority sisters as to whether I would ever graduate. At one point, she was the only person who believed that I could or would do it; at some low points I doubted it myself. However, my personal cheerleader Lorraine was right there with words of encouragement. Or when necessary a good kick in the butt and a remember you owe your ancestors speech.

I went to work for Los Angeles County. First for the Department of Public Social Services (DPSS), next for the Probation Department and I finally found my niche at the Sheriff's Department. Years passed. I had a successful career, but still something inside was missing. That inner desire was still burning within me. My dream was unfulfilled.

During this time, Lorraine had moved across country, married, and became a mom and career girl. How ironic, she always wanted to be the career girl and I had wanted both; career and family. Isn't it funny how life works out, she was married and I was still single? Her life was thriving and mine was stalling. Never once did she put me down, she just kept me encouraged.

When Lorraine and her family moved back to California, I was elated. I had a surprise for her that I had not shared with anyone, not even my family. I had enrolled in school. Returning to college as an older working adult is difficult at best. You're dealing with fresh faced youngsters who wonder why you are there. Also when you are working either at the county jails or at a patrol station it is extremely hard. Getting off to attend class was not easy. While working at the women's jail, I had to makeshift trades or use my vacation time. But I was determined that I was obtaining that diploma, that was my goal. During that time, the Department was not student friendly. However, Lorraine again was my biggest cheerleader. I finished undergraduate school with honors. I then immediately enrolled in a Master's Program. I was working on a graduate degree and she had now enrolled in law school. We encourage each other. Lorraine was now a wife, mother, career woman and law student. Her plate was full.

My plate was full. I was working in patrol, dashing from robbery calls, bar fights, domestic violence calls, drug busts, car pursuits and dealing with over-bearing supervisors who did not share your love of education. All of these could happen during the course of one shift. Most of the time I was dead-dog tired, but I hung in there.

Again, against the odds, we both succeeded. We graduated the same week. Lorraine with a Jurors Doctorate and me with a Master's of Science and both of us with honors. Fortunately, we graduated on different days. We were able to attend each other's graduation ceremony. Guess who were the loudest people in each ceremony? She was for me and I was for her.

I am now happily retired and loving life. I am travelling, doing speaking engagements and taking fun classes to keep the grey matter working smoothly. I am also writing a novel of my own and ghost writing a book for a singer. Not bad for two little girls from South-Central Los Angeles that main stream American had so easily written off.

EPIPHANIES

Lorraine and I are classic examples that it is not where you come from that determines where you go in life. Determination, tenacity, faith in God, belief in self and the support of a wonderful friend can conquer all obstacles. Indeed, we truly are *Friends for Life*.

Daily Prayer

Dear Father God,

Please give me,

The strength,

The courage,

The wisdom,

The knowledge,

The energy,

The skills,

The patience,

And whatever else is required,

To go forth through this day,

In Jesus' name,

Amen.

Darla Jackson

To: Baby Juan,
thank you for your support!
Blessings,
Darla Jackson

Darla Jackson

Darla Jackson

Is a writer with a passion for the public and the essential services she helps administer to them. With a Master's Degree in Public Administration, field experience collecting United States Census data and over 21 years of experience as a Public employee, Darla shares life stories to help better the lives of others. Darla's observation and experiences during her employment in the public sector spurs conversation through thought provoking topics. Darla is a freelance writer including poetry, with accomplishments in academic writing, including research studies resulting in findings and written reports through a myriad of resources. Darla is a member of Reflections Writers Society in Southern California and can be contacted by e-mail at: darladoright@yahoo.com. Telephone: (323) 627-0602 & 451-3330

The Call

Darla Jackson

"Darla, telephone" her cousin yelled. Darla leaped up, ran into the bedroom, and grabbed the phone.

"Hello this is Darla."

"Hello Darla this is Charlene Burley the supervisor who interviewed you at the State of California. I'm calling to see if you are still interested in the Office Assistant Typing Position." *Wow is this really happening?* Darla became anxious and her heart began to beat faster.

"Yes" she replied.

EPIPHANIES

"Well good, then I would like to offer you the position."

Without hesitation, Darla replied "yes!" I will accept the position."

"When can you start"? Ms. Burley asked.

It was 1992 and Christmas was in just a few days and it was Darla's favorite time of year. You see there were plans already in the making to pull over night parties the week of Christmas with some of her good friends as she had done the past few years. Starting a new job a couple of days before Christmas would definitely have put an end to this years' holiday social time with her friends. Realizing that Ms. Burley was giving her an option of when to start, she quickly answered "December 28th." This is when her journey into Public Service began.

Darla was so happy to get the job. She had worked hard to prepare for a new career that would help to meet her goals of becoming responsible and independent. In 1989 she started with enrolling in a rigorous word processing program offered by the NAACP, and later enrolled in an ongoing typing class at a local occupational center in Los Angeles.

EPIPHANIES

Public Service always interested her because many of her family members had success working for the civil service, and by observing their success she felt it was the perfect occupational field for her. There were also benefits and unlimited opportunities to elevate a person's career and these were some of the main reasons this type of employment was at the top of her list. Darla needed something that would help her provide all of the essential things needed in life. She was late in "leaving the nest" as some people call it, but she felt that starting this job would be a fundamental part of achieving her independence. And it was too! She moved into her own apartment six months later!

When Darla started working for the state she began working in the insurance department in policy services. Charlene placed her at a desk with another employee who would train her on her very first task of maintaining logs at the fiscal desk. She wanted to make a good impression so she would ask questions anytime she felt it necessary, because she wanted to get the task down and show that she was ready to move on to the next task. Darla's new co-workers were nice but she didn't feel an instant connection with them. She felt her new supervisor Charlene was nice and was a people person. She was a mid-sized young lady who came to work every day dressed the part of a supervisor, always well groomed in nice skirts or dresses and pumps. Darla was several years older than Charlene but she felt a connection with her. In the hiring interview, Charlene told Darla that she would be hearing from her. Darla knew from experience that when managers interview applicants they sometimes say that they will be in contact with them or you'll be hearing from them. Darla didn't know what to think but Charlene was right because she called her back into the office to take a typing test. After Darla took and passed the typing test it was just a waiting game before she got "The Call."

Before working for the State Darla had previously been employed through temporary agencies while taking vocational courses, and while working in other offices she always took pride in dressing professionally. Always accustomed to office dress, when Darla began her new position for the State her attire consisted of two piece skirt suits that her grandmother made for her. The fitted suits were tailored to her shape and they were unique because no one else had any like them. Once in a discussion in her new office regarding dress, Darla expressed the pride she had in the fact that her grandmother made her clothing, and a co-worker said "I don't like homemade clothes." After her co-worker's comment, Darla felt hurt and offended but she didn't react to the comment she felt was being directed at her. Darla's best guess was that this was a way of telling her that they didn't like her clothes.

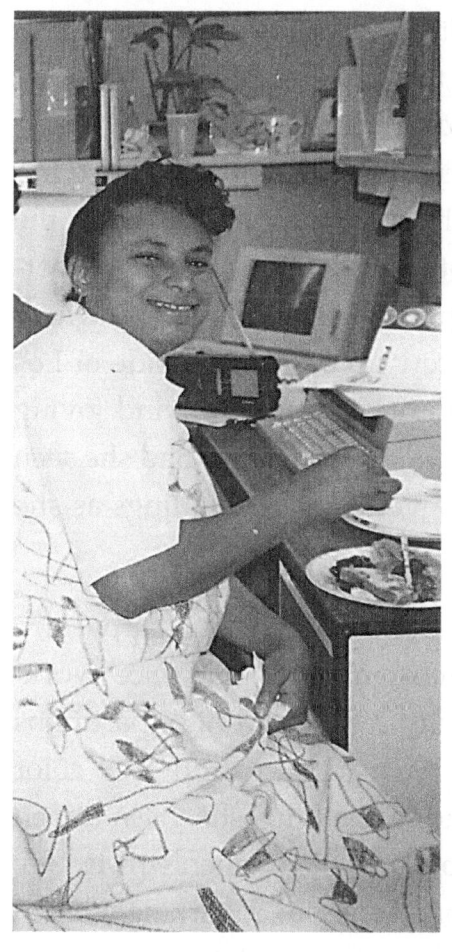

Homemade clothes, huh, Darla thought to herself. Well, whatever you want to call them Darla knew that if you had good taste, homemade clothes were the best ones because they are unique, one of a kind and made to fit in whatever color and style that you prefer. Not the taste of anyone else. In the office there was no dress code but the professional staff who worked in the field and those in the office who had meetings or walk-in appointments were expected to dress as a professional. Darla and the other office assistants didn't have the burden of dressing in other than ordinary blue jeans. The office had a professional but relaxed culture and communication flowed openly within the policy department. The work atmosphere was fun and relationships among staff members were cool. Darla and other employees including Charlene often spent time partying together after work hours. As an employee in the 1990's, Darla was not only thankful to have a permanent civil service position, she was happy where she worked. Darla grew up on the East side of Los Angeles near South Park. It was a fun and loving place to live with her family, but never had she seen such beautiful and convenient surroundings as she did on Wilshire.

Her new job in Civil Service made her happy. Inside of the office each employee had nice workstations or cubicles with carpet and high partitions for privacy with an ordinary pink and grey color scheme and they had something she hasn't seen since those days; a couch in the women's restroom. It is placed there in consideration of working women who needed a break due to their body's functions, or new and expectant mothers who were in need of a break to relax and regroup. It was nothing wrong with it but apparently it has been a discontinued practice. After working in the insurance department Darla never saw that courtesy again. It was practiced widely in the past because Darla's mom worked as a public employee since the 1960's and on a regular basis she told her that she enjoyed this convenience in the departments where she worked.

Being at work was like an amusement park at times. Staff could walk out of the building and instantly be in the mix with all the amenities they needed. The office was in the heart of the city on Wilshire Boulevard and many offices and buildings were occupied by celebrity companies. Darla once saw Heather Locklear star of Melrose Place a popular television drama in the 90's, and Sylvester Stallone and Sandra Bullock (stars of the action movie Demolition Man and many other recent movies,) filming in the courtyard of the building.

The building was one of what was referred to as "twin buildings" because there were two of them with a beautiful courtyard in between them. They were built with what was referred to as "real marble and granite" by the younger group of employees.

EPIPHANIES

Many buildings only cover the facade of the building with these expensive materials but these buildings had it featured entirely inside and out and when you walked down the lobby it felt as if you were walking through a Royal Palace! It was a beautiful area with many stores, a park owned by the building that was adjacent to the courtyard, good eateries, and celebrity sightings often, and the screen actors' guild was directly across the street and not forgetting to mention it was only five minutes away from Darla's home!

Darla knows that there is much to achieve before her duties in civil service are fulfilled. She will continue to strive to meet all the challenges that life brings. That's a step up from the old Darla and she calls it progress. She doesn't think back about those days on Wilshire often but when she does she knows that she has become a better person and civil servant because of her beginnings as a public employee

EPIPHANIES

Expression of Love
Darla Jackson

In Memory of
Alice Piccola Estes
08/19/1906 - 06/28/1998

"I love you Grandma. Through the years you've taken care of my sister and me, as if we were your own daughters."

"You have always been there for us when we needed you. I know I have picked up some of your ways, and many times I do and say certain things just as you would."

"I've realized how powerful love really is. Love can mend broken lives, and love brought you into my life."

"I thank God for the blessing of having two mamas, and I feel proud to say that you are one of them."

Choices

Darla Jackson

Love isn't something that just falls out of the sky,

If you don't feel loved and you ask yourself why,

It's something that all people desire,

But it isn't easy to reach or acquire,

If love is something you feel you deserve,

But you feel like you've been kicked to the curb,

Remember you have to give love freely and abundantly,

And not just sex, time, or money,

Because being no more than someone's whore,

You're gonna wind up, used, unloved or uncared for,

You get what you give and if what you give is easy,

Then you're not seeking love just a fantasy,

Love isn't easy but it's good as it gets,

Embracing the chance of it you'll never regret,

So hold up your head, pray and take the first step.

*I am enough, I have enough,
There is enough, always.*

As I move along my pathway in life, I am held in the embrace of Divine Safety and Security!

3/29/14
To: Baby Jace
Best Wishes!
Beverly HR

Beverly Hyman Reynolds

Beverly Hyman Reynolds

A native of Washington, D. C., Beverly received her undergraduate and graduate degrees from Howard University. She taught English in public schools and the University of the District of Columbia (formerly Federal City College). Her teaching career continued in Houston, Texas and Los Angeles, California. After her retirement, she began free-lance writing and editing. She is an avid reader and is inspired by American writers James Baldwin, Margaret Walker, Toni Morrison, August Wilson and John Grisham. Her strength is writing the short story which tells of her own experiences and her observations of the life journey of others. Her work in progress consists of a collection of stories, essays and poems entitled *Thought Pieces*.

Mama Afterwards

Beverly Hyman Reynolds

I heard her coughing as soon as I opened the door. She was gagging and could not catch her breath. I dropped my two wash loads in the hallway and ran to the den where she usually waited for me every Saturday. It was an early November day, a rainy and chilly Saturday, so I was glad to have Mama's warm house to do my washing. Yet I was scared that Mama would go into a stroke or something the way she continued to cough and gag. I got her to hold up both her arms while I gently rubbed her back. I didn't know what else to do. Gradually, she caught a good breath and began to calm herself. Her face was flushed and she coughed a few times without gagging. Then she took a really deep breath. I was relieved.

"Mama, you've been smoking again!" I tried to be calm.

"Just one," she whispered, looking at me as if to apologize. "I'm glad you got here, baby. I thought this was IT."

I looked her in the eye. "You promised me to stop smoking and see the doctor."

"I will, baby girl, I will." She sounded resolved, but then she added that word she knew I hated to hear. "Soon."

We both enjoyed my "wash day" visits. While my clothes washed and dried, we'd have tea and I'd listen to Mama talk about my growing up days and what a piece of work I was. Sometimes we both nearly cried on the bad parts, but then we'd sometimes laugh until we cried on the funny parts.

"Mama, I'm so glad you got me into boarding school; it was the best for the both of us. I got the environment I needed, and you got the freedom to finish school yourself. You didn't have to worry about where I was and what I was doing. Thank

EPIPHANIES

you!" Mama cried and stretched out her arms to hug me. I went to her to get that hug and to give her one. We hugged for a long time; then we laughed at each other as we dried our tears.

"Those nuns took charge of you, girl," she'd tease. "That first year when you came home for Christmas and I saw you clean your room without me having to yell at you a hundred times, I knew the sisters had you under control." Then she'd throw her head back and laugh out loud. Her laughter made her cough some more, but it wasn't as bad as what I'd first heard.

On my next wash day at Mama's, I found her strutting her stuff to Aretha Franklin's recording of "Respect." She loved Aretha and as she would adjust the 45 rpm to play the song again, she'd say "Aretha tells it like it is - respect when I come home!" Then she'd wait for the record to start again so she could do her dance.

Mama had persuaded her older sister, my Aunt Mabel to visit us for the Thanksgiving weekend. Aunt Mabel and Uncle Russell lived in Washington, D.C. and neither were fond of flying. But, they agreed to join us and teased about being Californians, deserting the Nation's Capital."

EPIPHANIES

Mama was Aunt Mabel's baby sister, and often bossed her. So I thought that was why Aunt Mabel was coming out. She also warned Mama about smoking so much.

Mama was excited. She'd already called a maid service for what she called a "good" house cleaning, and was planning her menu and guest list. It amused me to hear her talk to herself as she made plans to call her friends, neighbors, Bridge Club buddies and co-workers to invite them to Thanksgiving dinner to meet some of our family. I even contributed to the expenses, and when Mama saw my fifty dollar check under the dining table centerpiece, she smiled her "I'm proud of you" smile and winked at me as a thank you. I was proud to do this for her.

As I left with my bags of cleaned clothes, I turned to make certain I'd closed the door securely, when I saw Mama turn her back and reach in her robe pocket to pull out a pack of cigarettes. I immediately went back into the house and to her surprise, took the pack away from her. "This is what's making you cough so badly, Mama! You are killing yourself!" I was screaming. She sheepishly promised to quit smoking "soon." "When's that, Mama?

EPIPHANIES

When is *soon*?"

"Right after Christmas," she said softly, reaching for me to hand her back the pack of Virginia Slims. I didn't give them to her. I took them with me to throw in the trash bin at my place, realizing my gesture wouldn't work. Mama knew where in her house she could find another pack.

Later that night, she called me. "I'm dying... get me to the doctor!" I rushed her to Emergency; the doctor took one look at her and said she might have had a heart attack. He was right. It was a really bad one.

When Aunt Mabel and Uncle Russell got to California, it wasn't for Thanksgiving dinner. They came to attend my mother's funeral.

It was hard for me to understand that my mother was dead. I had some sleepless nights and after all the rituals and gatherings were over and everyone had left. I worried and cried my eyes out. I wondered where she was and if she were in a safe place.

"Where are you Mama?" I cried out loud. "Are you okay?" "Dear God, where is my mother?" Then one night as I prayed to God that my Mama would be

EPIPHANIES

alright, I experienced three consecutive dreams - each on a Saturday that told me what I call, her redemption. I realized they were from her to tell me otherwise what she had always believed and said out loud many times. **"When you're dead that's it, baby. You're done!"**

~~~

It seemed as though I had come to visit her, and I waited in a beautiful garden, surrounded by a knee high brick wall. When she emerged from a haze, she was accompanied by what seemed to me a man-like figure wearing a long white robe. He had long hair and showed no expression and stood behind her, but gazed directly at me. Mama walked toward me, and I realized that we were separated by that brick wall. She stopped at her side of it to face me. She wore a wide brimmed hat and a long skirt. Her breasts were bare. She was angry.

"Are you all right, Mama," I asked tearfully.

"Well, I guess so," she shouted angrily and rolled her eyes.

"Are you sure?" I asked.

"What did I just say, girl?" She shouted again.

"I just wanted to know, Mama. I'm sorry ...I'm sorry."

"I'm sorry too!" she complained. "They tell me I died, dammit! And I had plans!"

EPIPHANIES

At this point the gowned figure put his hand on her shoulder. Mama turned towards him and began to cry. I thought he meant to comfort her, but he was taking her back into the haze. I could think of nothing else to say to her as she walked away, and she didn't look back. I cried to get her to look at me, Mama! She was gone.

~~~

I was in her kitchen searching for the casserole dish she would lend me. As I pulled it down from the cabinet, I saw her sitting at the kitchen table. Seeing her surprised me since I couldn't imagine how she got there.

"Mama?" I gasped.

I could tell she answered me, but I could not hear her voice, and that reminded me that she was dead. She continued to talk while gesturing, nodding, shrugging her shoulders and finally, putting her hand to her chest and patting it. I saw her sigh and I felt it myself. She stopped talking and I could tell that she wanted to stay and talk some more, but instead she rose from her chair to leave. She tried to smile, then walked into a haze right at the kitchen door that led to the backyard. This time she turned to look at me and blew a kiss. I cried and cried and cried.

~~~

EPIPHANIES

We were in the kitchen again. This time Mama was exuberant. Again, I could not hear her voice, but I could tell that she was talking and it was incessantly, joyful and excited. I was happy to see her dancing and clapping her hands. She threw her head back as she laughed, something she did when she was alive, to show me that she was happy. I got happy with her as if she were alive and just visiting me. After those few minutes of being joyful, she seemed in a hurry to leave. So she blew me a kiss and turned to go and began running toward the haze. I called out to her as she rushed to where I saw through the haze a path that led to a hill. On each side of the path were two large dogs, sitting like the Sphinx in Egypt. I rushed after her. I called, "Mama" knowing how fiercely afraid of dogs she had been. But as she passed them she showed no fear and they accepted her taking the path. There was no barking, no chasing.

But, as I approached the path, believing that I could help my mother, the dogs stood and blocked my way to the path. I was afraid they were going to attack me, and I braced myself, anticipating the pain of their bites. They didn't bite; they gently nudged me away from the path.

~~~

Mama's love made those dreams for me so that I'd know she was alright. She had progressed from anger to acceptance to joy, and her two dogs showed that she was protected and was in a place where I was not yet to go. That made me so happy. My mother had indeed died, but she was most certainly not done.

*Every day is a new beginning, and I release,
let go of, learn from and forgive the past.
Allowing the living waters of gratitude to
flow freely through me like a
blessed eternal river, relaxing, refreshing,
renewing and reinvigorating,
every aspect of my being.*

Leaving Houston

Beverly Hyman Reynolds

I moved to Houston, Texas in the early 70's to teach at Texas Southern University to get what I called a "new" experience living in the South; an adventure I dared to call it, in these United States of America. I participated in civil rights activities in Washington, D.C., and thought that a real life experience in Texas would deepen my appreciation of *The Struggle*. What I had not realized at the time was that I was a militant and expected some racial incident at every turn in Houston. I was verbally armed and ready for any such thing should a *white versus black* incident occur. What a surprise it was for me to live, work and socialize in the Houston community

EPIPHANIES

among the Hispanics and whites without a single encounter of racism. The salespersons in the department stores were cordial, the clerks at Texas DMV were courteous and helpful, and the mixtures of the races at some community gatherings were open and genuinely caring and visionary. The most southern of drawls were the most liberal. Why even the policeman who stopped me to issue a speeding ticket called me ma'am and even said nicely, "Thanks, you drive safe now," as he handed me the citation. Nothing that I can recount in the three years I spent there was mean or racial. None... except when I was preparing to move to Los Angeles.

My mother had been living in Los Angeles with my stepfather for nearly ten years. She loved California and often called the place God's Country, and encouraged all our relatives on the East Coast to move to California right away! She convinced me that it was time for me to live near her too, especially since teaching jobs were plentiful, and she thought it was time for us to live closer. Besides, I enjoyed her warm sense of humor and her love for me, her "baby girl." And I needed that comfort. She said she'd picked out a "nice" fellow my age to marry, and I hollered laughing. All that along with her claim

EPIPHANIES

that she considered herself the best mother I could ever have. So, I decided to move to Los Angeles.

Travel "light" was my mantra as I began selling all my furniture and household stuff. An ad in the Sunday paper led to frequent calls and visits from friends and strangers. I was thrilled that things were selling fast and I enjoyed the one instance when one of my close friends competed with a neighbor for my living room furnishings. My neighbor won by twenty dollars!

In the flurry of throwing in sheets and towels, dishes, pots and pans to sweeten some sales, I flew to cloud nine and perched there. Everything was going well; I would sell everything, pocket the money and be on my way to California. This move was just peachy, and it was only three days before I was to leave with only my dining room set to sell.

I was alone when the call came from a woman who inquired about my ad. In her remarkable drawl she said she wanted a dining room set, and boy did I appreciate hearing that. "What a happy coincidence," I exclaimed. "It's a beautiful white French provincial six piece set and I'll be glad to....."

She cut me off, "Oh, my lord, are you a nigger?"

EPIPHANIES

Cloud Nine abruptly pulled out from under me, and I tumbled into the abyss of reality.

"Are you a nigger?" the woman impatiently asked again.

"What?" I asked in disbelief.

"I said are you a NIGGER!" she shouted.

I was shocked, and slammed down the phone. My heart raced, anger rose in me and I could feel heat crawling up my neck. I nearly choked just trying to breathe. My heart was still racing when the phone rang again. Was it the hateful woman or was it another customer? I took a chance and answered in hopes that it was someone else.

"Hello?" I tried to be calm.

"Hello, nigger" she sang. "You got some *fun-nit-chuh* to sell me, nigger?" She laughed. I hated her.

I was quiet for a few seconds, and in that short time, my mind recalled the stories told by my Virginia and North Carolina families about their struggles to stay alive and not lose faith despite the murders, the mutilations, the humiliations, the lynching, the rapes and the half white children and

EPIPHANIES

the shame of families who had to raise them. I recalled tales of the terror of night riders, of lingering Jim Crow laws, and the tales from slavery with old "Massa" our white ancestor or "Mr. H" as he was called, who regularly held great Aunt Patsy hostage in the big house to have his way with her. Then it struck me, I had the trump card.

"Girl," where is your man this evening? Has he left you alone at home with nothing to do? Are you bugging me because he's gone and you don't know where he is? Well, I can tell you where he is, girl. He's with his *nigger woman*, that's where! He's with that beautiful golden brown skin thing he just can't keep his hands off! You know what they say about white men just LOVE-ing those nigger women. Of course that's supposed to be a secret, but it ain't no secret, now is it? You *know* what I'm talking about, girl, now don't you? Don't you!" I screamed into the phone, my heart still racing, and I'm still furious.

She said nothing.

"Hello...hello?" I called, getting bitchy with her. "Are you there Miss Lonely White Trash?" I shouted, still angry and ready for her counter-attack.

EPIPHANIES

No reply.

"Hello?" I shouted again into the phone. "Now did you want to buy my dining room fur-ni-ture or not?" I loved my sarcasm and meant to end this madness. Then I heard the dial tone. Miss Lonely White Trash had hung up. But my heart kept racing.

On my flight to Los Angeles, I thought about that phone call, and actually prided myself on how I got down so quickly on that racist gal and struck her right where she lived. I told her the truth and hit a nerve. I had to realize that the past is still the present and that even in the best of environments, there is the dark side.

So, I did indeed have my adventure in the South, and I began humming that civil rights melody, We Shall Overcome, wondering, *shall we really overcome? Will we ever?* I took a deep breath and decided to take a nap.

Oh! I never sold the dining room set. It sat unbought in the apartment in Houston as I flew to Los Angeles.

The Seven Minute Story
Beverly H. Reynolds

Can you imagine writing a story in seven minutes? Well, I'm here to tell you it's entirely possible. That is, if you have a good memory. Our writer's workshop leader challenged us with this exercise after several sessions on what the writer should seek to accomplish. So there we sat, some of us frowning, others of us with blank looks on our faces, and still others starting to write immediately without any trouble at all. Well, that was not me. I had to labor for at least a minute to find a memory based on the leader's theme, "I Remember When." What a challenge!

EPIPHANIES

"Where Gently Flows the James"

I remember when in my junior year in high school, Sister Timothy, our principal, lead all the classes to chapel to pray to the Holy Ghost -it was a "ghost" in the 1950's--to help us pass our final examinations which were to start in two days. The freshmen appeared to be grateful for the opportunity, since it was well known that the rigors of the 9th grade classes were the hardest ever experienced in our school. The sophomores looked a bit arrogant, because by the end of the school year, none of their classmates had dropped out, and they had the impression that they knew everything there was to know about anything one would want to know. On the other hand, some of my classmates and I were a bit fearful since our year was the year with Sister Rene, the terror with geometry. She could teach it in her sleep. Of course Louise and Judy, the smartest in our class, had no problems with math.

The girls in the senior class were the most anxious, however. All they wanted was to graduate. They were divided between getting married right away, or going to business school to get a "good" job, or to go on to college.

EPIPHANIES

So, there we all were in chapel, kneeling on the wooden prayer benches, heads bowed and hands together with fingers pointing upwards praying to the Holy Ghost to make certain that we all passed our exams; and for me, I prayed to avoid going to summer school. After the Rosary and the three *Glory Be's*, we filed out silently from Chapel to return to our respective homerooms.

I was the first to get to ours. There was Sister James Mary, our homeroom teacher, standing at the door, arms akimbo, frowning and impatiently tapping her left foot, waiting for us to get into the room so she could fuss at us about something. I wondered what infraction my classmates and I had committed this time.

As the last of the "Sweet 16" got into the room, Sister announced "We have just insulted the Holy Ghost!"

"Huh?" "What's she talking about?" We looked around at each other, puzzled by what Sister had just declared.

She began calling on some of us.

"Judy, do you have the books you need?"

"Yes, Sister," Judy giggled, "All of us have our books."

"Beverly, where are your glasses?"

"I'm wearing them, Sister.

"Margo, do you have yours?"

"Yes I do, Sister."

"Dorothy, can you read?"

"Yes ma'am...uh Sister."

"Velma, do you remember what you read?

"I sure do, Sister!"

"A show of hands, who in this room can't read?"

No hands went up.

"Who in this room is without everything she needs?"

No hands again.

"Who in this room is able to hold a pencil and write?"

All hands went up.

"Margo, are there study periods at this school?"

EPIPHANIES

"Yes, there are, Sister."

"Alice, when are our study periods?"

"Every day, Sister, from four pm to five-thirty before supper and from six-thirty to eight forty-five after supper during the week. AND, Alice continued, "from p.m. to p.m. Saturdays and Sundays in the library or in our homeroom.

"I see." Sister paused then started again. "Who in this class does not spend time to study?"

No hands.

Sister stood quietly, just looking us, "I see," she said again. "Well, it's time for the bell; get ready for your geometry class." The bell rang as Sister walked to the door, opened it and stood there watching us file out. There was no expression on her face. What was wrong with her today?

It wasn't clear to any of us why Sister quizzed us this way. Was she upset? She didn't appear to be, and we knew that it's normal that we would go to chapel and pray for help when we were in need.

At supper, we all talked about the entire scene in homeroom, but no one had a clue. We thought maybe Sister was just having a bad day. Nuns did that. One day they were happy and calm, and the next day they seemed irritated and mean. Go figure.

In study period the next day, Judy sat across from me as we searched for answers to our American History study guides. She leaned forward and whispered to me, "What are you smiling about?" I never answered her, but it had dawned on me what Sister wanted us to understand. We should not have worried about passing final exams or any exams for that matter. While going to Chapel with prayers for help was embedded in us, we should know that our books and our eyeglasses and our ability to read and write and the planned study periods at school were the gifts that the Holy Ghost had already given us. All we needed to do was to give God our thanks and just buckle down to study.

Amen?

This story is dedicated to the Sisters of the Blessed Sacrament, in memory of Sister James Mary, and to my class of 1956 "mates" at St. Francis de Sales High School located in Powhatan County, Virginia, affectionately known as "Rock Castle."

Pamela Snowden

Is a writer who now lavishes her creativity on inspirational writing instead of on legal briefs. Pam practiced law for many years, and has worked as a consultant in various areas since moving on from the practice of law.

Pam enjoys her family life with her life-partner Isabelle. Their adult daughter Jolanda still is very much a part of the family even though she works, and travels extensively, from her base on the East Coast.

Pam's spiritual journey from believer to atheist to agnostic to woman of faith now has come full circle with her ordination as an interfaith minister. Pam writes to offer hope to her fellow human beings through the message of the availability of spiritual empowerment as a path to satisfying life. Pam can be reached at AskRevPam@aol.com. She'd love to hear from you!

Lost and Found

Pamela Snowden

My friend Jean and I giggle nervously as we pull into the parking lot. At 16, we are just old enough to have drivers' licenses. The parking lot is large and parking is easy which comforts a new driver like me. Jean and I get out of the car in silence and walk slowly up to the entrance of the building. Neither of us moves. The oversize double doors trimmed with woodcarvings and inlaid with stained glass dwarf us. I take a deep breath as I reach for the door handle. My hand looks tiny on the brass handle. I have to put my entire weight into pulling open the door. My heart is as heavy as the door.

The receptionist smiles professionally. "May I help you?"

EPIPHANIES

I take another deep breath. "We're here to see Saundra Harding." The receptionist checks a list.

"Saundra is in Room 3, down the hall on the right. Would you like me to take you to her?"

Jean broke her silence. "No thanks. We can find it on our own."

Saundra had been our buddy, and we are making this journey to view her body on our own, without adult assistance. We stop at the door of Room 3, taking time for our nervousness to subside before we enter the room where our teen-age friend's body lies in a casket.

We move timidly into Room 3. The stillness in the room is the stillness of Saundra's 16 year-old corpse lying in a casket. Jean and I stand on opposite sides of Saundra's casket, each of us lost in our own thoughts as we study her body in the casket.

A powerful wave of sorrow washes over me as the finality of death takes hold in my mind and my heart. Saundra looks like herself, at least on the surface, her body is there, but my dear friend Saundra has left us forever. My silent scream echoes in my mind, *Pam, why have you been going to church all of these years? You were a proud youth leader, getting dressed up and walking to our neighborhood Presbyterian Church every Sunday even when no-one else in the family goes with you...why? It's all lies and foolishness. Death is final and forever and religion is full of crap.*

That night I lost my faith, my faith in a loving, just, all-powerful God who watched over us and protected us, His beloved children.

Many years have passed since the sorrowful night at the funeral home. I am sitting in church, reluctantly, at the behest of Isabelle, my partner of many years. I have attended services a few times with Isabelle, who has become one of the faithful. There have been many changes in my life over the course of those years, but one thing that has not changed is my negative attitude toward religion, an attitude that fluctuates between indifference and outright antipathy.

The format of the services is familiar to a service at a Christian Church, but the doctrines are drawn from a wide variety of sources, including but not primarily the Bible. The formal name of this institution does not contain the word "church." The general term used to describe this religious philosophy is "New Thought." I find the New Thought approach to matters of faith more palatable than traditional religious doctrines but I have no interest in attending formal services on any regular basis.

The pastor delivers his sermon. *I sure hope the sermon doesn't last too long.* I fight the urge to fidget in my seat. I struggle to keep my focus on his words rather than on my worries, on the "if-onlys" and resentments that monopolize my thoughts. I maintain my focus long enough to hear the words that change my life.

"Most of us are not fully awake in our lives. We are so worn and distracted by the cares and concerns of our daily lives that we feel trapped, without options and at the mercy of circumstances. What we need to do is to wake-up to the truth of who we really are! We are emanations of the Divine and we can use the power of the Divine within us to take charge of our lives, create options for ourselves and live the lives we want and deserve. "

I snap to attention and sit up straight in my seat. He is speaking directly to me! He is reading my mind and my heart. His words of spiritual wisdom reverberate through every aspect of my being. The blazing sun of hope rises in my soul, illuminating

EPIPHANIES

the faith that had lain dormant all these years. What was lost now is found. I was blind, but now I see.

Within 2 years of that day when I found my faith, I released myself from the trap of self-pity, creating new options for myself and for my life, and embarking upon the path that led to my ordination as an interfaith minister.

Today is graduation day. I stand proudly in my ministerial robes with my fellow interfaith seminary graduates on the stage in the beautiful neo-gothic sanctuary of the historic Riverside Church in New York City. This church is famous as a focal point of national and international social justice activism, and has been for the entire 80 years of its existence. We stood on the same stage that Rev. Martin Luther King, Bill Clinton, Nelson Mandela, Paul Tillich and Reinhold Niebuhr, among others, stood, addressing the congregation and the world.

We look out from the stage into the faces of our families and friends who fill the sanctuary. The spiritual director of the interfaith seminary moves along the stage engaging each graduate in turn. After what seems like an eternity, it is now my turn.

EPIPHANIES

The spiritual director smiles into my beaming face and hands me a white rose. I accept it gratefully. "Reverend Snowden. Please recite your vows of ministry."

"I, Reverend Pamela Snowden, vow to live my life as an expression of the God-qualities of Faith, Hope, Truth, Love, Joy, Happiness, Beauty, Creativity, Generosity, Courage and Compassion in my life, the lives of my friends and family, and in the lives of all those beings with whom I come in contact."

My spiritual journey now has come full circle. The loss of a friend took away my faith. The words spoken by the pastor restored my faith. The pastor's words cleared the internal fog that clouded my awareness of the Divine Spirit within me and within everyone. We are one with each other and one with the One Spirit in us, as us, is us. One with Spirit, all is well!

*I am grateful for the material and spiritual
wealth that I enjoy.*

*I live, learn and grow with the joyful expectancy
of discovering new talents and abilities within me.*

*I move onward and upward, awake and aware of
the limitless possibilities of my life.*

Affirmations

Pamela Snowden

*I am fully supported, richly blessed,
happy and at peace.*

*I am enough, I have enough,
there is enough, always.*

*Every day is a new beginning, and I release, let go of,
learn from and forgive the past, allowing the living
waters of gratitude to flow freely through me like a
blessed eternal river, relaxing, refreshing, renewing
and reinvigorating every aspect of my being!*

*My unlimited potential meets every demand in new
and expanded ways.*

I learn and grow from any seemingly missteps.

*I move forward with my day in confidence
and in calm expectation of success.*

*Powered and guided by my inner divine
I overcome any challenges.*

EPIPHANIES

I move through the day with joyful confidence.

I inhale energy, enthusiasm and optimism, and exhale worry, doubt and fear.

I focus on the truth of the mental, physical and spiritual well-being of my divine self.

I am fully prepared to overcome any seeming obstacles to creating the life I want and deserve.

I am eager to demonstrate my masterful life-skills.

I establish and enjoy a prosperous rewarding, lavishly-compensated career with excellent benefits doing productive, fulfilling work in congenial environments, with skill, strength, determination and success.

As I greet the new day I take deep and invigorating breaths.

*I breathe in the joy of new beginnings.
I breathe out the burdens of the past.*

*I breathe in vim, vigor and vitality.
I breathe out the illusion of powerlessness.*

*Satisfying solutions exist to the challenges
I face. These solutions are within me
even if I am unaware.
I know that these solutions will come into
awareness and manifestation in God's good time.*

Mel Taylor

Is a marketing expert, and owner of Circle One Enterprizes, a successful marketing company. Mel is a licensed Spiritual Practitioner and has helped many in their walk to a higher self-realization. Mel is an active member of The American Legion, and is co-publisher of Reflections Publishing House. He resides in Los Angeles, CA. Contact him at: meltaylor2001@yahoo.com.

We Walked With Tears in Our Eyes

Mel Taylor

"I have some very sad news for all of you, and I think sad news for all of our fellow citizens, and people who love peace all over the world, and that is that Martin Luther King was shot and was killed tonight in Memphis, Tennessee. Martin Luther King dedicated his life to love and to justice between fellow human beings. He died in the cause of that effort."

Excerpt from the impromptu speech on April 4, 1968, by Presidential Candidate, Senator Robert F. Kennedy

Thomas came running fast down the outdoor walkway right after school screaming. "Man, you

EPIPHANIES

heard? Martin Luther King has been shot and killed by a white man. I got to get home!" I stopped in my tracks, stunned, not able to move. Tears flooding my eyes, my knees felt weak, I sat down on the bench, in shock on that overcast April afternoon at Washington High.

The school campus emptied quickly, but I couldn't move. Students and teachers rushing by me, and I just sat there in disbelief and sorrow. I slowly began to recover as I absentmindedly thumbed through my notebook filled with stories I had written about the latest on the Sanitations Workers Strike in Memphis. African-American History was my favorite class and I was eagerly learning about black people and the civil rights movement. My God…

Suddenly out of nowhere, appeared my good friend Cheryl Bradbury. She was bloodied and her blouse was torn, tears streaked with mascara running down her cheeks. She had a painful looking knot rising on her forehead, her white knuckles and knees where scrapped and bloody and her long red hair standing up all over her head like it had been pulled. She felt into my arms scared, crying "you got to walk me home, please! I don't want to get into another fight!" I didn't say a word, as she handed me her books, straighten her plaid dress, took my arm, and we left the campus grounds. Cheryl had been attacked by some upset black students, taking their

EPIPHANIES

anger and frustration out on her because of the color of her skin.

Washington High School had a handful of white students, a growing black and Mexican population, and the Asians were a quickly dwindling majority. There had been a few racial incidents that I had heard about, but this was the first time I'd been even remotely involved. Those rare incidents were usually between Mexicans and African-Americans.

As we walked, Cheryl saw me crying and wiped a tear off my cheek, and said defiantly "those damn guys that attacked me got a few licks and scars too, they got their nerve," trying to cheer me up. "Yeah, they don't know you like I do, you are one cool white girl," I replied smiling through my tears.

On the first day of school that semester I was surprised to see Cheryl sitting in the front row of the Black History Class. A white girl in school studying black history back then was unheard of. She told me History and English where her favorite subjects and she knew very little about black history, and wanted to know as much as she could. I knew Cheryl was a straight A student so hanging out with her was an added plus for me. We sometimes did our homework together in the school library, and talked for hours on the phone about school and other things.

EPIPHANIES

Our conversation as we walked was mostly about Dr. King and all the wonderful things he had done for the civil rights movement, the March On Washington, the sit-ins, going to jail, the marches. We also talked about the riots that gripped Los Angeles a few years back in 1965 and other violent events we had witnessed or read about.

Our mile and a haft walk to Cheryl's front door was coming to end as we were approaching her house Her mother, Mrs. Bradbury, peeked out the window and rushed out the door, horrified at the condition her daughter was in. "What happened to you?" her mother asked, hugging her and looking questioningly at me. Cheryl quickly introduced me while explaining what happened and I was invited in their house where the news was on TV.

Senator Robert Kennedy was giving a speech about Dr. King's assassination. The news afterwards showed footage and stories of riots going on in cities across the country in the aftermath of the assassination. As I was watching the news I thought about how we are all so interconnected as I looked at Cheryl and her mother sitting on the couch weeping.

To this day, I still have highest regard and respect for the legacy of Dr. King, his relentless dedication, his courage and leadership during those years of the civil rights movement, speaks volumes. He

EPIPHANIES

brought to our awareness the means to begin a healing of the deep racial divide between blacks and whites. He taught and preached that love was the answer, the common thread that could build a country that worked for all, based on brotherly love and respect.

It was getting late and time for me to go home. Cheryl graciously thanked me for being there for her and her mother grabbed my hand in appreciation as she looked deep into my eyes thanking me for walking her daughter home.

As I walked home on that cool cloudy Thursday evening the sun was going down in the west, reflecting on my thoughts and the spectrum of emotions shown by others, I walked silently, mourning the tragic death of a phenomenal man on that April day many years ago.

I will give thanks to the Lord with all my heart

Psalms 9:1 (NASB)

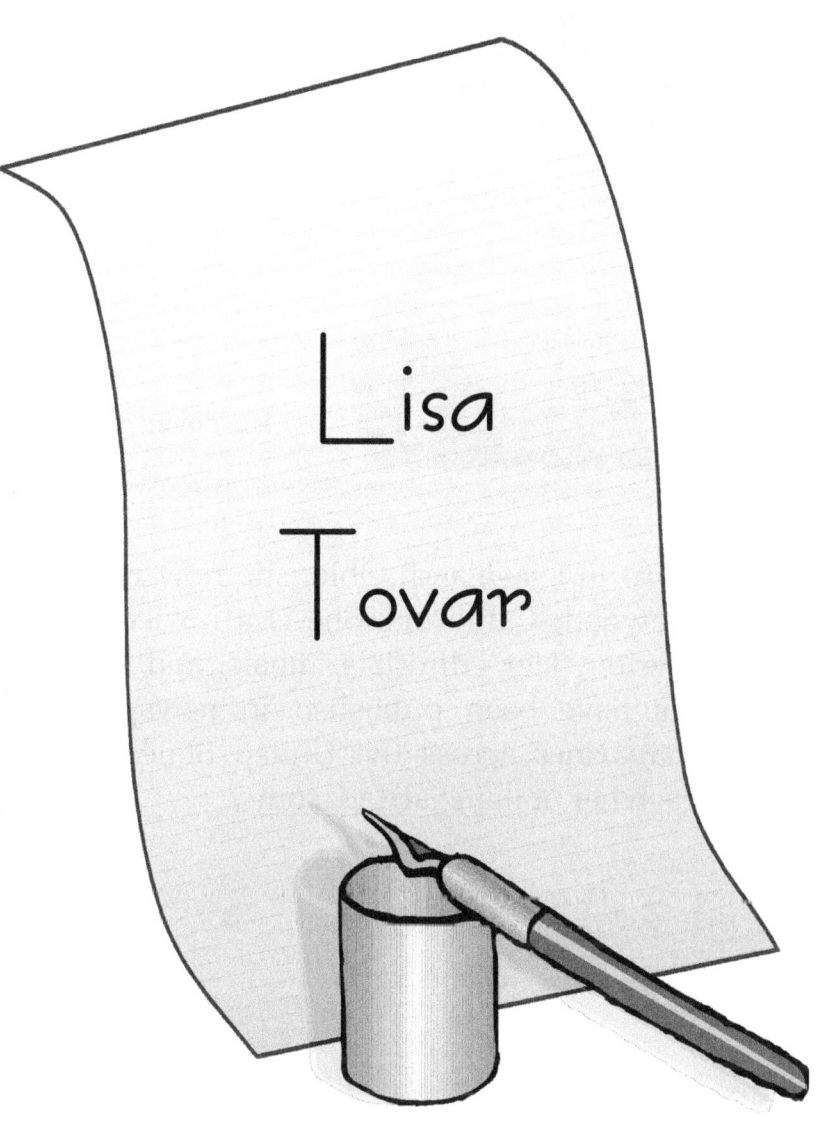

Lisa Tovar

Was born in Cleveland, Ohio; she now resides in Inglewood, California. She is a novice freelance writer. Her editorials, music, and article reviews have been published in newspapers and magazines across the United States. You can reach her at llaniciat@aol.com

The Skin That I Am In

Lisa Tovar

The other day when I overheard a woman describe someone as "high yellow," the hair on the back of my neck stood up and my insides started to cringe. I found myself getting angry, hearing those two words brought back some painful memories.

My family is a rainbow coalition. Our skin colors range from fair to a golden dark brown. I was raised in Cleveland, Ohio. My mother was Negro and my father was Mexican. I was the third of five kids. Mama and Daddy always said, "We should not judge anyone by the way they looked on the outside." Therefore, in our household, skin color was never an issue.

We were brought up in a *"mixed"* neighborhood where people didn't care if you were bi-racial,

EPIPHANIES

purple or green, as long as you weren't crazy, they would accept you with open arms. Back then, all the kids got along; we played hopscotch, baseball, double-dutch rope, and hide and seek. But my favorite game was kick-the-can. I loved hearing the words "ally-ally I'm free." This meant that I could come out from my hiding place without losing the game.

Our parents didn't have a lot of money, so we were creative, especially when it came to having fun. There was a huge, weeping willow tree in our yard; we found a long rope, wrapped it around one of those thick branches, tied an old car tire to the bottom of the rope and we were good to go. Kids from all over the neighborhood would line up just to swing on that old tire.

Summer came to an end, and it was my first day of school. I remember sitting in my rocking chair, as Mama combed my hair. She slapped some Royal Crown grease on my ends (to make sure they wouldn't curl up), then brushed my hair back, to make two tight ponytails. Once I was fully dressed, she looked at me, with that beautiful smile, and softly whispered in my ear "Lisa, you are a pretty little girl, but always remember, pretty is as pretty does." She placed her index finger on my heart and added "but it's not what's on the outside of a person that matters… it's what's on the inside that

EPIPHANIES

counts, and don't let anyone make you believe any different."

I was only five; I didn't know what she was talking about, in a rush to leave for my first day of school, I just said, "okay Mama, I'll remember." Looking back in retrospect, I think Mama knew what may lay ahead for her little girl.

I loved everything about school; the teachers were nice, I was a straight "A" student and I had plenty of friends. All through elementary school life was good. I was in a loving family, I was happy; I didn't have a care in the world. I was a little girl enjoying her childhood.

But then everything changed. My parents separated; Mama had to get a job; we had to move out of our house. I was heartbroken. We were going to leave the only community that I loved and knew so well. Nothing could have prepared me for what I was about to experience.

It was the summer of 1962 when we moved into an apartment that sat above a storefront church, in a tough, low income, all Negro neighborhood. This was a neighborhood where folks didn't seem to like newcomers, especially, if they looked different.

Without getting to know me, the kids immediately,

EPIPHANIES

labeled me as "The Outcast." I tried to make friends with a few of the girls but they were not having it. One girl had the nerve to ask me where my real mama was. I guess she thought a woman with dark skin couldn't possibly have a child with light skin. I was hurt. Tears filled my eyes, and I ran in the house. It was awful.

Here I am, a teenager, hormones jumping, face breaking out in big red pimples, my body taking me thru changes that I didn't understand and, even worse, I did look different from everybody else.

Most days I would sit on my back steps, all alone, sulking. But I couldn't get away from them. They would gather in the parking lot below and start shouting out names like; "high yellow, half-breed, mutt, albino, and ole yeller." Those words were painful to hear. Scared and confused, all I could do was run inside and cry, like a baby.

Whenever I would have to walk to the store there would always be a group of girls hanging out somewhere near the store and without fail, one of them would shove me, call me something like a "yellow heifer" and dare me to say anything, because if I did, they would kick my butt. I didn't open my mouth, I was scared. I would just pick up my pace and hope that I would make it home without having to fight.

EPIPHANIES

I think I spent most of my early teen years crying and running. Crying because of the painful names the kids called me and running because I was scared.

I didn't talk much about what was going on inside of me because I was embarrassed. I was beginning to feel like I was all those things that the kids called me.

One of the few times that I did talk to Mama about what was going on she told me about those "sticks and stones," and reminded me that kids could sometimes be cruel. Then she repeated those words she had spoken when I was five, "It's not what's on the outside of a person that matters…it's what's on the inside that counts." That wasn't what I wanted to hear. So from then on, I internalized my feelings.

I'm not sure how my neighbor Carol and I became friends but we did. She was my savior. But at the end of the summer Carol and her family moved away, never to be heard from again.

I started junior high school and, on the first day, all of my fears came to life. The bullies that had teased and threatened me for the past three months were right there, all in the same building.

For two semesters, I ran home from school every

EPIPHANIES

day. And every day there would be, not one, but several kids on my heels, calling me names like high yellow, chicken and pale face. My only wish then was that I could wake up to dark skin and coarse hair.

Finally, tired of running, I decided that I was going to walk home for a change. I hadn't made it very far, before I was surrounded by a crowd of kids, shouting, "get her; get her, get her." Then, out of nowhere, a girl named Pricilla, ran up to me and punched me in my jaw. I can recall seeing stars, all colors and all sizes. I heard her say "now what cha gonna do…you, yellow belly?" I just stood there; I could hear laughter and the words fight, fight, coming from the crowd then someone shoved me into Pricilla, and the fight was on.

The next thing I remember was the owner of the barber shop breaking up the fight and saying to me "girl, you gonna break my shop window with that girl's head. You kids stop all this nonsense and go on home."

The next day, in school, everyone was talking about the fight. It seemed that I had earned my badge of acceptance. The next few weeks were mind boggling for me. The kids were actually talking to me and not about me

EPIPHANIES

It wasn't long before I started hanging out with the *wildest* and *toughest* girls in school. I started smoking, drinking, cursing like a sailor, and ditching school; I was on a downward spiral. I don't know how I passed to the next grade, but I did. I just thank the lord that my mother never found out about my outrageous behavior.

I was in the ninth grade when Mama came home, and announced that we were moving. One of her co-workers managed an apartment building that was in a nice, middle income, predominantly black community. All I could think about was the fact that I would have to start all over again; a new school; a new neighborhood; a new everything. I was angry. But as life would have it, the move proved to be one of the best things that could have happened to me in my teen years. It got me back on the right track.

It wasn't easy; it was the 60s, it was during that time the "Black is Beautiful Movement" began. The words I'm black and I'm proud were being bellowed by blacks throughout the United States, race-related riots tore through many black communities. The afro and dashiki was being sported by blacks everywhere. And despite constantly being teased, I wore my "fro" and with my fist raised high, I too shouted, "I'm Black and I'm Proud."

EPIPHANIES

I now understand, people are going to do what they do, say what they say, and it is up to me, to accept it or reject it.

I can let others determine my self-image or I can choose my own self-image. I have those choices.
Even with that knowledge, I still despise those derogatory words used to describe African Americans with light skin. To me, it's like a Caucasian using the "N" word.

Slowly and painfully I have come full circle with who I am, as a person, and…"I love the skin that I am in." Thanks Mom, it took some time, but I finally got it!

> ***Before you were ever formed in your***
> ***Mother's womb,***
> ***I saw you and approved you.***
> ***Jeremiah 1:5***

Paula White

Also known by friends as Pepper, is a budding author of inspirational stories of survival. She was born in South Central Los Angeles, CA and is the seventh of ten children. She has a natural gift for fashion and spends time volunteering with young girls, teaching them style and self-respect. She has an upcoming book entitled, From Felon to Fabulous, which gives step by step instructions to anyone striving to have a purposeful life after serving jail time or being convicted of a crime. She can be contacted at blessedpep@gmail.com

So Not Stupid

Paula White

I was having one of the best days I've had in a long time. The sun was shining brightly, I had the top down on my car and the heat felt great on my skin. That's one thing I love about living in California, its January and its 80 degrees outside.

I had just finished doing my all-time favorite thing, shopping. I had been looking for the perfect pair of black boots. I went to the Fox Hills Mall; and a store which is usually too costly for my budget, had a pair of boots that were just what I needed. I went in expecting to window shop, but found the boots on sale at a price I could afford.

Yes, this was a wonderful day. As I drove home, I dreamed of the night I would have. I'd planned a quiet evening alone. I loved to read and I had

EPIPHANIES

purchased a new book so, my great day was now going to be an even better night. Suddenly my cell phone rang. It was my daughter Mia, Mia is 26 and she's a flight attendant. She lives in 3 different places; sometimes she lives in Hawaii, with her best friend. Sometimes she lives in Los Angeles with her boyfriend, but mostly she lives with me.

She said, she was at her boyfriends and asked me to come pick her up. Well, so much for my night alone. It was alright though, Mia had been on a 7 day trip and she had been missed. When I picked her up; she got in the car and was a little quiet. Sometimes, after a long trip, she's tired and doesn't talk much.

She took out her cell phone and showed me a picture of a baby. She said to me, "Look at this ugly baby." I replied, "I don't think the baby is ugly at all." I did think it was rude of Mia to make a comment like that about an innocent baby. Mia continued to talk about the baby, "Look at her big lips, this baby is ugly." I told her how I had contemnplated having some filler put in my own lips to make them fuller.

EPIPHANIES

All of a sudden Mia snapped and said. "You sound so stupid, you don't make any sense. Oh what, are you a white women now? You are so ungrateful, you should just be thankful for what you have. Stop trying to be all Hollywood."

I was in shock and just couldn't believe that my child would talk to me in that manner. Never would I dream of speaking to my mother like that. She'd knock me into next week for even looking at her wrong. But I wouldn't ever hit my child. Thinking about it now, *maybe I should have*. Because here she is yelling at me and being disrespectful.

Mia hurt me to my core. I was so mad. I had to pull the car over and get out. I walked down the street a bit mumbling cuss words and trying to convince myself not to ring her neck. I couldn't believe her. I got back in the car and started to drive home. I was still very upset and had thoughts of driving into oncoming traffic. But I didn't want to kill us or anyone else for that matter. I just wanted to erase that entire conversation with her. I wanted my Mia back, not the one that had shown me that picture. My Mia loved me, and was sweet and kind. She didn't talk like this person. We had our problems, but this was something very different.

When we finally made it home, I told her how much she hurt me, and how she would never be al-

EPIPHANIES

lowed to be disrespect me again. I waited for an apology, but none came. She didn't say anything, and when I asked for an apology, she said, she thought this whole thing was an overreaction on my part. Wow, she's got some nerve. I later found out that the baby was that of Mia's boyfriend. A man she had been dating for over two years and had hoped to marry someday.

She needed to stay out of my way for a while. Even though she was hurting, she still didn't have the right to hurt me. I felt dizzy so I lay down on my bed trying to figure out why I was so upset by being called stupid. After all that word had been used so often in my life. Momma used to say it to me daily. She would say my sandy brown, nappy hair, looked dirty and no matter how much Murray's hair grease she put on it, my edges still wouldn't lay down. Unlike my six sisters who all had long, good hair just like Mommas. She'd say I walked stupid because my legs were bowed and I had to wear braces for years to correct them. She would laugh when I got tangled in the blankets at night and would fall out of the bed.

The teachers and other students called me stupid in school because no one knew I was dyslexic. I remember spending a lot of time crying alone as a child, I was quiet and didn't like being around too many people because after being told I was stupid

EPIPHANIES

so often, I believed it. After all a mother wouldn't lie to her child, would she?

Even later in life when I married. I got pregnant and the doctor told my husband and me that we were having a boy. My husband was so excited, he spent hours painting the room blue and decorating it with footballs, baseballs and all kinds of trucks. On delivery day, out pops Ms. Mia screaming with all her might. That was one of the many times I'd allowed him to call me stupid. I didn't care about what he had to say about me, secretly I wanted a girl. No matter what she looked like, I would love her with all my heart and be proud of my daughter. I was just happy she was healthy. That was probably the first day I believed I had finally done something right.

One day when I was about six, Momma told Daddy to help me get dressed. Daddy didn't like to help me much. He said I was too fragile and he might hurt me. He did enjoy doing things for my sisters though. He'd say how they all looked just like his favorite girl, Momma. He called my sisters' L A's Finest. In our neighborhood of South Central Los Angeles, that's what they were known as. People would point at them when they walked down the street, everyone loved them. On the few times I was allowed to tag along, people would ask if I was really their sister.

EPIPHANIES

Daddy used to say I belonged to the mailman. I was too young to understand what he meant by that. I did notice that the mailman was very nice to me. But then again, he was nice to everyone. He had sandy brown nappy hair like mine and his eyes were light brown like mine also. I used to think maybe there was some special, magical place that he and I came from. I would wait for him to come deliver the mail, hoping he would do or say something so I could get some kind of understanding on why I was so different from Momma and my sisters. But he never did, he just delivered the mail.

Well that day when Daddy was helping me, something strange happened. As Daddy was putting on my shirt, he stopped suddenly and grabbed my arm. He held it tightly and looked at it closely. He looked in my eyes and back at my arm. I thought I had done something wrong and was going to get a spanking. I was so scared I was shaking. Then I looked at my daddy, he had a tear in his eye. He just kept staring at my green birthmark. It had always been there, Daddy had just never paid that much attention to me before that day. Then Daddy showed me his arm, he had to same green mark and in the same place as mine.

He held me real tight for a long time. I could feel his heart beating fast and he was breathing hard, almost like he was hurting. I felt warm inside,

EPIPHANIES

happy and loved. I felt special. I was special. I had Daddy's green mark. None of L A's Finest had that. I had finally found a connection to someone. Daddy became my world and from that day on, he never mentioned the mailman to Momma again.

Daddy and I would go places together and he would hold my hand and show people our green mark. I would act like I was better than my sisters. It didn't hurt quite as much now when people talked about me. But it did hurt. As the years went by I learned to embrace my nappy light brown hair and when I walk you can hardly see my bowed legs.

So why, after all these years when my daughter said that word, that word that is nothing close to who I am. Why does it still hurt so much? Well no more, I refuse to give it any more power over me. I choose to live the rest of my life knowing that I'm strong, I'm smart, I'm beautiful, I am special, not just because I have my Daddy's green mark but because I'm SO NOT STUPID.

*Powered and guided by my inner divine
I overcome any challenges.*

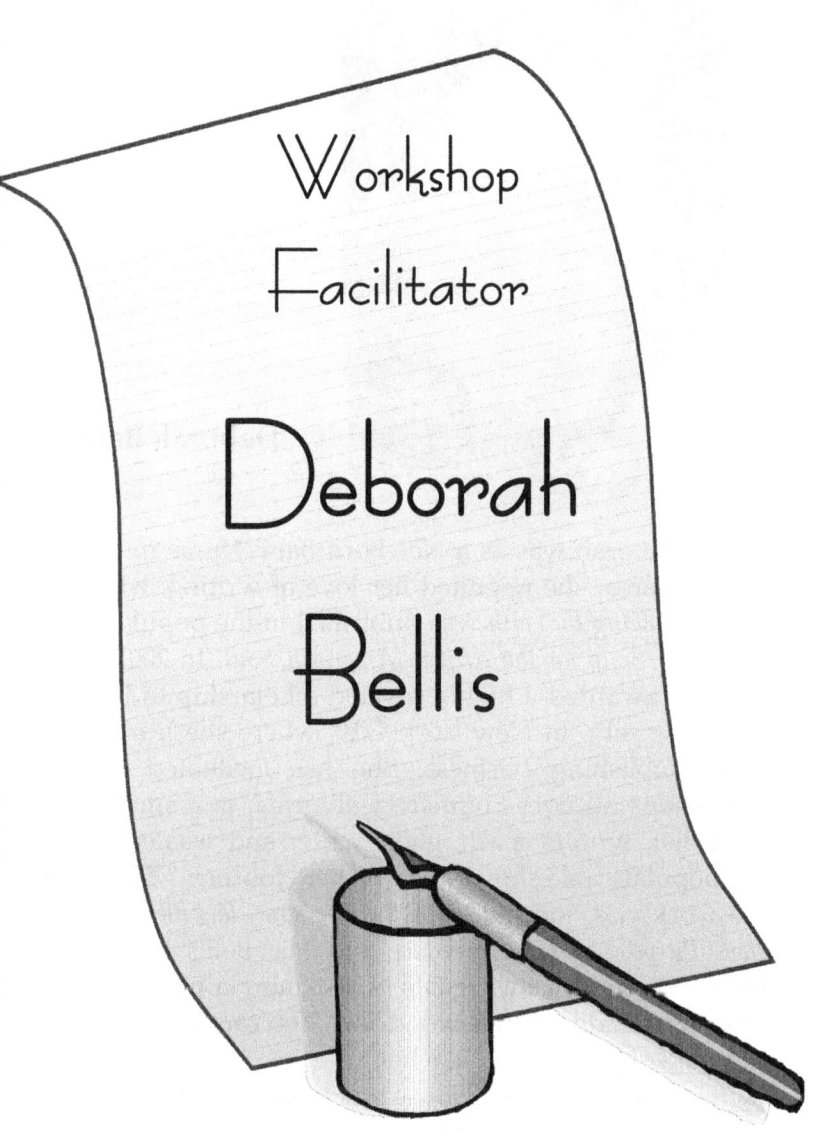

EPIPHANIES

Deborah Bellis

While Deborah was as a Newborn Baby Nurse in the Los Angeles area, she reignited her love of writing, when her story, *Walking by Faith* was published in the popular book, ©*Chicken Soup for the African American Soul*. In 2007 Deborah was awarded a highly coveted scholarship to Publishers University, in New York City, where she learned the book publishing business. She has facilitated writers' workshops all over Southern California, is a small press publisher, writers coach, ghost writer and was co-host of the popular cable show, "The Writers Journey." She wrote the workbook/journal, *Breaking Writers Block through Passion, Purpose and Perseverance* and Ms. Bellis has helped many accomplish their goals of becoming a published author. She resides in Inglewood, CA. You can reach her at dabellis@sbcglobal.net; like her at Reflections Publishing House on Facebook; website address is reflectionspubishings.com or visit her blog at; reflectionsph.blogspot.com.

Hit it

Deborah Bellis

Mama loved Las Vegas; I had a timeshare so we went quite often. We went by every mode of transportation, plane, train, bus and car. If we needed to cross a body of water to get there, we could have added boat to the transportation list. Often it was just the two of us, other times it was a car full of family or friends, or a few cars driving in a caravan.

Somehow, driving through the desert, in April 2005 my mother sitting patiently next to me, I sensed that this would be the last trip we would take together. Six years earlier, she was diagnosed with a stomach aneurysm. The doctors said they could perform surgery, but warned us that the surgery

EPIPHANIES

was risky and recovery would be extremely difficult. There was nothing else they could offer, so, without the operation, it was terminal, and they gave her six months to live. Mama wasn't interested in any surgery, so all she asked when she heard the news was, "can I still eat what I want?" We all had a good laugh. I took her to her favorite restaurant and life went on.

I loved my mother; she was my best friend, my biggest cheerleader, my angel and my rock. I lived in a sunny spacious apartment with a big porch that Mama loved and when my roommate moved, I asked if she wanted to live with me.

I wondered how I would manage, I was scared. I really didn't want the responsibility of caring for her, but I knew in my heart that it was the right thing to do. Mama was a little reluctant, but she came around and a few months later, she moved in.

It was a trying time. We clashed many days, struggling to find our way. Watching my vibrant, exciting, loving mother decline was not easy. We made it somehow with God, humor and the love and support of our family and friends.

Oh, but, how Mama loved Las Vegas. "What time are we leaving?" She'd ask, flushed with excitement. Mama loved the lights, the pace and the vibe

EPIPHANIES

of that town. She was always anxious to hit the slots right away, she'd play for a few hours, then she was content just sitting somewhere watching the sights and hearing the sounds of the town.

This trip was different; we shopped, went sightseeing, caught a Las Vegas show, and treated ourselves to an extravagant dinner. On the second day we went to get Mama's two hour slot play in. "I feel lucky Deb" She told me and off we went to find that winning slot machine. We found it. It was one of those new ones that rose high and had many levels.

I pushed Mama's wheelchair close and put in a few coins, and after playing for only a few minutes, I got a spin. We were so excited. I gave her instructions, "okay Ma, when you say 'hit it,' I'll hit the spin button." Soon we were on a roll, every spin yielded some money, the machine was hot, a crowd was gathering and Mama was yelling, "Hit it!"

I will never forget the look on my 81-year-old mother's face, sitting next to me yelling "Hit it!" She transformed right before my eyes. The pain and suffering were gone; the years just melted away. And just for a few minutes she was a young girl again, grinning, laughing and happy. Mama sat there cheering me on, clapping her hands, enjoying the attention and living for the moment. In a flash

EPIPHANIES

all the hard work that we had gone through, all the frustrations and sadness that we felt, all our fears of death and dying was gone. We were free.

Mama slipped away five days later in her bed as I watched her take her last breath. Her face and body relaxed, she looked so peaceful, and I felt calm in my soul. I stood there for a while, smiling behind my tears because Mama had just hit the big one. She was going home, she was free and flying with the angels and I was glad.

EPIPHANIES

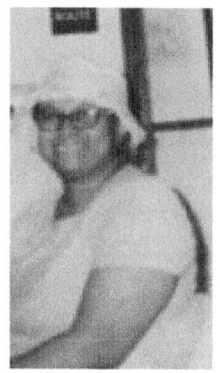

EPIPHANIES

CPSIA information can be obtained at www.ICGtesting.com
Printed in the USA
BVOW11s0834060314

346864BV00002B/2/P

9 780979 213243